THE COST
—— OF THE ——
WIN II

Reflections of My Journey
and What It Cost to Win

TAMARA LOFTON

authorHOUSE®

AuthorHouse™
1663 Liberty Drive
Bloomington, IN 47403
www.authorhouse.com
Phone: 1 (800) 839-8640

Published by AuthorHouse 12/20/2018

ISBN: 978-1-5462-7350-9 (sc)
ISBN: 978-1-5462-7349-3 (e)

Library of Congress Control Number: 2018914969

Print information available on the last page.

This book is printed on acid-free paper.

Contents

Reflection

I identify with Chapter 10; "What I need is already in my hands." When we begin to utilize our skills, we are not aware of what can be produced. The "still small voice" is always ready to assist when we start the process. We are sometimes surprised at the results in the finished product, be we know that we did not accomplish it alone. Thank God for using what we have in our hands to do great and miraculous things! Eld. Beverly Jones. Stone Mountain, Ga.

Dedication

It takes a village to raise a child.
It takes a village to shape by example.
It takes a village to promote good character.
It takes a village to stabilize integrity.
It takes a village to produce a leader.

To the "Village"
Willie M. Strong(Madea), Mr. James Lee Griffin Sr.,
Deacon Leonia & Eld. Beverly Jones,
Pastor Ulysses Purdy,
Bishop G.E. Patterson, Apostle Gail Patterson,
Ms. Love Bowie,
Bishop J.D. & Lisa V. Wiley-Taylor,
Mrs. Carrie Tigler,
Prophet Wilbert & Debra Ayres,
Pastor Bill & Dr. D'Ann Johnson,
Eld. Theresa Gilstrap, Eld. Gordan Graham,
Pastor Fred & Margaret Caldwell,
Dr. Winton & Eld. Lavern Robinson,
Dr. Toni Alvarado, Apostle Richard D. Henton,
Rev. Victor Belton

These eagles shaped my life and taught me to soar. Although bruised along the way, they displayed their scars as trophies of honor. Consistently engaging in the good fight of faith, they realized that "winners never quit and quitters never win".

They recognized His voice,
responded to His call,
and responsibly completed each ordained assignment,
teaching me to do the same....

If I Could Teach You

If I could teach you,
I'd teach you how much more you have
accomplished than you think you have.

I would show you the seeds you planted some
years ago, that are now coming into bloom.

I would reveal to you the young minds
that have expanded under your care;
the hearts that are serving others because
they had you as a role model.

If I could teach you teacher, I would show the
positive effect you have had on me and my life.

Now you have a homework assignment;
It is to know your value to the world
To acknowledge it and believe it…

Dedicated to Ms. Sergeant
By: Byron K. Smith
Irving Elementary School Class of 2012

Introduction

From sunrise to sunset,
From dawn to dusk,
From the first morning punch of the time clock,
until the last punch at the close of day,
"He daily loads us with benefits."

This chapter is dedicated to all of the provisions received
and desires granted to me through the years.
I am so grateful having a new respect for
(Matthew 6:11 and Luke 11:3).

Chapter VIII

Daily Bread Daily Benefits

- Bread-
bread was sacred; considered a gift of God…
His continual and undeserved care,
familiar and accessible to all….

-Benefits-
bounty, avail, profit, magnanimous

Give us this day our daily bread
(Matthew 6:11, Luke 11:3)

Blessed be the Lord who daily loads us with benefits
(Psalms 68:19)

"I stopped complaining when I began to take inventory
of the Lord's daily provision. Then I realized His
benefits were a tangible fulfillment of His promise."

I invite you now, to walk with me, thru
some noteworthy experiences of
"Daily Bread and Daily Benefits."

"*Divine Protection*"

I did not make a public confession of salvation until the age of eighteen, but I vividly remember an encounter of the Lord's divine protection, "a daily benefit", when I was only twelve years old.

I had just gotten off the bus and walked the half block to our apartment building. I was just across the street and about to step off the curb when a car pulled up in front of me. I proceeded to go behind the vehicle and it backed up. When I tried to cross in front of the car, it quickly pulled up preventing me from crossing the street. There were several young men in the car laughing and teasing me. This awkward process went on for quite a while. I remember thinking how my mother and my grandmother, always told us to come straight home. If we didn't obey, something might happen to us. Here I was right across the street from our dwelling place, and couldn't get to the driveway because of these inconsiderate teenagers.

I remember thinking in my head, Lord, I came straight home, but if you don't protect me right now, being obedient, just won't be enough to get me across this street. I need you to watch out for me! I need your help! I need you to protect me now! At that exact moment, the car quickly accelerated and raced down the street. I ran across the street, down the driveway, and up the twenty-three stairs to our second-floor apartment. I didn't tell anyone about what had transpired but I never forgot that encounter.

"Creative Provision"

One landmark event occurred while living in Memphis. During the summer of 1982 my income was a meager $50.00 per week. After paying tithes and a few small bills, I had only $3.00 left. Back then I always shopped at the same grocery store. I was a little bit hungry that particular day but felt lead to patronize a different store in the same chain. Something very miraculous happened while making my food selections that day. Many of the items were buy one get multiple items free. When I left that store, I had two full bags of groceries. Remember now, I started with only $3.00 in my possession. When all purchases were scanned and bagged, I also received change back. I've never forgotten that experience and thank God often for His miraculous provision.

"New Course- New Plan"

While sitting with my mother in the hospital, I lost my purse. The process of replacing driver's license, debit, insurance, and membership cards was minimal. The most challenging part was that the two USB ports used to store all of my original book ideas were in there as well. There was no back up to replace six years of work, or so I thought at the time. Amazingly, I was reminded that I had printed a few pages of the original outline. While reading the outline, the Lord changed the entire format of the book. New ideas flowed freely. What was lost became background research. A new format and direction was birthed and I successfully completed the assignment; "The Cost of the Win" Part I and II.

"Bill Provision"

Very close to the holidays, the utility bills were unreasonably high. Rent was due, and the car note was two months behind. I didn't panic, but I was very concerned. Quieting myself, and pondering these things in my heart, I engaged in major negotiations.

Favor prevailed with my vehicle lienholder. Most of the utility vendors granted extensions, but the Water Authority attempts were futile. They insisted that I pay the entire past due balance on the Monday, immediately following that same weekend.

After gathering money from all expected sources, there was still a $40.00 deficit. Provision prevailed! By Monday, I was able to pay the Water Bill in full with no problem.

"Food Provision"

Buying food during this financially strained-time, was totally out of the budget. What a blessing to receive bread, vegetables, meat, and sometimes snacks, from a neighborhood food pantry. The recipes inspired by the available provisions were so tasty. I was eating better then, than when I worked two jobs buying groceries on a weekly basis. Some weeks, surplus bread, and desserts were available. This was a double blessing for me, and a time to share with others. To be an active participant, blessing other families, in the midst of my time of lack, was priceless.

---Resourceful Provision---

Two years prior to this financial challenge, I purchased special TV antennas with the ability to transmit digital signals. When the cable service was discontinued, I plugged in the antennas. Instantly, I had thirty-three channels to watch.

With the internet also being disconnected, I utilized two alternative resources. The purchase of a Thesaurus at Dollar Tree substituted for Dictonary.com. Acquiring a free library card, gave me access again to the internet. Provision had already been made before the need arose to cut back on expenses. These inexpensive tools thwarted a potential set back in the successful completion of this book.

When you have resources flowing on a steady basis, invest in the tools that you may need. Continue in the path that He is leading you on. Don't allow excuses to prevent you from completing your assignment! Be creative! Seek wisdom, then gather the necessary resources.

Miracle Moving Provision

In 2016, my mom passed away, my roommate relocated to another city, and I was left with the entire financial responsibility of a six-bedroom house. Monthly resources dwindled while past due bills continued to soar. The decision to downsize and relocate was evident. I inquired of the Lord, and a house became available with less monthly expenses. The wheels were in motion and I had less than two weeks to pack and move.

I proceeded with arrangements; secured a U-Haul truck, transferred utility services, and secured manpower. I only had two men to help with the heavy stuff; refrigerator, washer and dryer, couches, beds, generator. Then I would drive home, take items to Good Will, clean and return the truck to U-Haul. I did this for two consecutive Saturdays. By the beginning of the third week I was exhausted.

On Monday, a lady came to view the property and saw me packing items into my car. Instantly, she offered to finish the moving dilemma for only $150.00. She had three boys, and her own U-Haul truck. What a relief that was and a sure answer to prayer. On the very next day, they helped me move the remaining items to the new location. They also took the final truck load of donations for me to the Salvation Army.

At that time, I only had $42.00 in my pocket and payday was not until Friday. She trusted me and accepted the partial payment. On Friday, I received my first pay check from my part time job. It was enough to pay the moving balance and to put gas in my car. The Lord provided a daily provision again and this moving exercise was complete before the Christmas Holiday. "And the sons of strangers will build your walls, and their gates will be open continuously" (Isaiah 60:10).

I needed to give away a twin bed and a bunk bed set including dressers. My first thought was to give it to the Goodwill but I needed assistance in taking the frame down. I offered it to several people but no one responded. Then I found out about a Deacon's group project to assist families with beds. Their desire was to accomplish this before the end of the year. My goal was to also be completely moved before the end of the year. They came to my house with tools to take it down and a truck to transport it. I became the bridge, assisting them with their project and in turn they assisted me with mine. You never know who will be placed on your route. God made the way again, where of I am glad!!!

When I first inquired about garbage service, I was informed that I would have to pay a past due fee of $88.00 in addition to the current bill. One month later, I finally had enough money to get the garbage service transferred. When I called to finalize the arrangements, I was told that I only owed $42.00. With great joy, I secured that payment. The service would be updated, activated, and ready for pick up on the following Monday. Then I inquired about the past due from our previous address. She researched the account and found nothing was past due. He provided a "daily benefit" once again!

"Transportation Provision"

In June 2015, my engine blew on I-20 W very close to downtown Atlanta. I didn't have a working cell phone at the time. After pulling the car to the left median, I prayed for the right kind of assistance. The police responded, called the Hero unit, and stopped traffic to push me over to the right shoulder of the interstate. They called a tow truck for me and the driver took me to the Kia Dealership in Austell, GA, very close to my residence at the time. After that episode, I went straight to Dollar General and purchased a prepaid cell phone. The phone was $4.00(a clearance item) and the minutes $19.99. This was a lesson learned. It adjusted my focus, prompting me to prepare for the unexpected. God still provided and met the need once again.

On another occasion, I found myself at the beginning of a work week, with ¼ of a tank of gas and no cash. After viewing a $-.68 cents bank balance, and with only $2.00 in change in the bottom of my purse, I needed a miracle. It takes at least $10.00 to fill half my gas tank.

I prayed for a miracle, and looked again. The bank balance was a positive $5.00. Did I rejoice! I couldn't wait to get off work. I stopped at the QT gas station on the way home, put that gas hose in my car, pressed the regular gas switch, and allowed it to pump until it stopped itself.

When I restarted my car, I had a full tank of gas! Daily Bread-Daily Benefit!!!

The most recent occurrence happened early on a Monday morning on my way to work. I hit a pot hole very hard on I-285W destroying my front left tire. I called on the Lord first, but then used that $4.00 prepaid phone, to call 511(the "Hero Unit") myself. The attendant quickly changed the tire, but the car still wouldn't start. He gave me a boost and told me there would be no charge. I was presently surprised, but was informed that as a tax payer, I had already paid his salary. By 8:00am I was walking into the front door of my job. Two hours had passed since leaving home at 6:00am, but I was very grateful and safe!

Part two of this adventure ended with even more victory. I took the car to "Tires Plus" where I had purchased two of my tires back in July. Thank God, I had purchased a full warranty, which lasted for the lifetime of the tire. The tire damaged in the episode, had just enough tread left to qualify for "totally free" replacement. After purchasing another warranty for the new tire for $11.00, I was offered an option to purchase lifetime warranties for the two remaining tires. These tires had been purchased from one of their competitors. I gladly agreed and now have four tires, with full warranties. This will be for the life of the tires, with free replacement.

I thanked the Lord for protection and for purpose. He already knew that I would hit that pot hole so hard, that the tire wouldn't hold up under the impact. He positioned my car and provided a safe haven to pull off the interstate with no obstructions in the way. God knew the lifetime of that tire was just about up. The tread on that tire would barely fulfill the warranty specifications and needed to be replaced anyway. He knew the stipulations of the warranty, and also knew that I wouldn't have to pay to replace the tire. I kept saying God, I don't understand, but you know the why, to the what, of this ordeal. Thank You for working it out for me. Once again, He did just that!

Several months after this, my battery stopped working twice. I didn't have enough money to buy a new one and pay day was not until Friday. This was just Wednesday, and I needed to get to my part-time job by 10:00pm that night. I called my Big brother expressing my battery issues and the concern to not get stranded at home if the car wouldn't start. He told me that I could wait at his house that evening before going to work, but meet him at Walmart first. They had batteries on sale and he would buy one for me and I could pay him on Friday.

I stopped by my house to shower and change but didn't dare turn off the car. I left it running in the garage with the door open. Then I drove from College Park to Decatur, Ga where he met me at Walmart. The service department closed early so he checked the size of the battery himself. He retrieved a trade-in battery from his car, went back inside, bought one of the batteries on sale, and came outside with a brand new battery. Mindfully following his directive not to turn off the engine, I patiently waited outside.

In minutes, he replaced my sick battery with a brand new one. He even had all of the right tools in a very concise case. I thought that we would have to charge the battery but it started right up. I was so grateful and relieved that I wouldn't be stranded late at night or early the next morning.

In 2018, I had been believing God to open a door into the Voice Over career. He spoke that thought to me as I relocated back to Atlanta in 2013. I had a few prospects but none of them panned out. One day in April 2018, I went to work as usual. There was a young lady waiting for me to train her. I didn't know that she was coming but I began her training any way. We began to talk and I expressed my desire to get into that business. She was an assistant to a booking agency and submitted my resume, professional photos, and samples of my voice work. That was the second time that the Lord brought my desire and placed right in my lap. Oh what a day of rejoicing that was!!!

For many years, I absorbed the word by merely digesting sermons that I'd heard across this country. Although this was a good start, I had to learn to exercise the word in my life. I learned not to stress out, but to pray, listen for instructions, then wait patiently. The application of "rhema," a Greek word that signifies the action of utterance:

- the Word spoken
- the Word revealed
- the Word executed

has been extremely valuable and the results simply amazing. The Lord has held my hand, and walked me through this journey called "life." I no longer live in fear. The Hymn "A Mighty Fortress Is Our God brings me much comfort. It is a constant reminder of His Daily Bread and Daily Benefits.

"A Mighty Fortress is Our God"
guard, protection, security, support, wall,

protection against external danger or annoyance

"A Bulwark never Failing"
wall of earth built for defense; rampart

Rampart
barricade, barrier, defense, elevation, fence

The Lord wanted me to know that He had me, guarding, and protecting me through every difficult experience. He is my fortress, support, defense, and citadel before, on the way to, and in the midst of my next assignment. I will accomplish my purpose and fulfill my destiny with the assistance of His

"Daily Bread, Daily Benefits."

Chapter IX

Responsibility Breeds Maturity

Responsibility-
make decisions of authority, control, power,
leadership, being accountable

Maturity-
coming of age, state of being mentally
and emotionally well-developed-
therefore responsible

"Arise, for it is your task, and we are with you;
be strong and do it" (Ezra 10:4).

"Whatever you find to do, do it well because where
you are going—the grave—there will be no working or
thinking or knowing or wisdom (Ecclesiastes 9:10)

"Responsibility is more than an obligated sense of duty.
It is a trusted example of accountability,
that blooms into a beautiful bouquet of seasoned maturity."

What is your level of obligation?
What does your accountability meter register?
What is within your power and control?
What are your managerial capabilities?
What does it take to push you into responsibility mode?

1st

Desire to take care of business….
2nd
*D*evelop problem solving skills….
3rd
Devise an *action* plan….

Parent Duty

Being the primary caretaker of both my parents required some pre-planning. An intense relocation process, and the acquisition of gainful employment were the first priorities. After submitting twenty-plus job applications, only one responded. I reported to work by June 10th, 2010, and the new assignment was well underway.

Moving in obedience to the plan, I expectantly watched the Lord work out all of the details. Within three years, that assignment was over and it was time to return to Atlanta. The hand of favor opened up again. I secured a position, and relocated back to Georgia. Surprisingly, my mother, who had been very reluctant, also made the move along with me.

-Project Building-

The process of selling our family building had been an interesting learning opportunity. Certain details had to be taken care of if we were going to collectively reap the benefits of our family inheritance. Financial situations were strained, and an unplanned absence from work was questionable. I had to be responsible, devise a plan, and execute a major moving exodus. Since my parents had both passed, our second floor apartment would have to be completely empty. The new owners wanted to assess and occupy it on closing day. The entire task had to be completed within a four day window.

- I arranged seven PTO days off work.
- Secured a discounted roundtrip airline ticket.
- Packed a small suitcase.
- Secured a two-man moving crew.
- Rented a U Haul truck.
- Disposed of fifty-three years of personal items from an upstairs apartment.
- Dispensed items at two different donation sites.
- Physically pushed all of the contents to employees who wouldn't help me empty the truck.
- Arranged for a professional mover to move a piano which had been sitting in the same spot for thirty-two years.
- Made a final trip to Good Will.
- Filled and arranged the disposal of fifteen large trash bags.

- Secured a temporary home for two antique chairs of sentimental value.
- Spent five extra hours at Chicago's O'Hare Airport in a potential snow storm.
- Returned to Atlanta at 5:00pm in enough time to make it to my part-time job by 10:00pm.

Extensive labor was required for this task. As usual, the weight of the assignment had been dumped into my lap with minimal assistance. Challenge, executed with excellence, was embraced with determination. Inconvenience and discomfort turned ignorance into knowledge as wisdom preceded the journey. Every minute detail had to be scheduled and executed from start to finish. Responsibility transitioned into maturity, and a profound occurrence took place. At journeys end vigor, strength, and an overcoming faith became the prize of the day. God blesses a struggler!

After you have suffered a while-
make you perfect(complete), established(stable),
strengthened(strong), settled(grounded).
(I Peter 5:10 KJ)

…so that the person who serves God
may be fully qualified and equipped to
do every kind of good deed.
(2 Timothy 3:17 NIV)

"Of much is given, much is required" (Mark 10:28 KJ)

"He has called us to suffer long but not always"

When you responsively step up to the plate accountability is formed. Responsibility develops strong roots. Engaging in challenges builds endurance, determination, and balance. This newly acquired strength gives assurance, durability, cohesion, and soundness.

Win by Being Responsible in Everything that You Do!
Maturity will definitely follow!

Chapter X

What I Need is Already in My Hand

HAVE-
to get, possess, receive, occupy,
latch onto, take in, team with, get hold of

HANDLE-
grasp, hold, seize,
enlarge, stretch, lengthen, strengthen

For His divine power has bestowed and given us:

- [absolutely] everything necessary for...AMP
  - everything required for....CSB
  - everything we need for...CEB

---life and godliness---

and

- has been miraculously given to us…MSG
- has already been deposited in us…TPT
- all this was lavished upon us… TPT
(2 Peter 1:3)

*"Need provoked me to access unknown, untapped resources,
to find the treasure within!"*

The inspiration for this chapter came from two sources. The first was a sermon rendered by our executive Pastor, Dr. D' Ann Johnson ("I Have What I Can Handle"). She admonished us to focus on, and cultivate the gifts that we already possess, rather than covet what we don't have.

Then I caught a glimpse of the magnificent potential of Bezaleel and Oholiab; (Exodus 31:1-6; 36-39), two very gifted men in the bible who were chosen by God to assist Moses in building the temple.

Bezaleel, son of Uri, son of Hur from the tribe of Judah,
means "in the shadow of God" or
"filled with the spirit of God."

Oholiab, from the tribe of Dan, means "tent"
of my father or my father's "tent."

Bezaleel, a master-craftsmen full of wisdom, insight, and knowledge, interpreted the vision that God had given to Moses. He possessed an ability to comprehend deeper meaning with understanding.

Both men came from a rich lineage of service in support of the work of God, ever mindful that every good and perfect gift comes from above. They possessed diverse skills in stone and wood design, and devised cunning works of gold, silver, and brass. The will of God was manifest in precision, expertise, and artistry, as they submitted to the task of God.

While meditating on this rich information, my life was impacted. God places common gifts within us. This raw talent, whether developed through educational pursuits, or cultivated through practice, is discovered when a proficient skill level is achieved. These untapped resources are to be utilized to create our best life.

Even though we labor to develop and mature these talents, they are not exclusively for our personal enjoyment. Yes, we have what we need to create and thrive naturally and spiritually, but we must realize that it was given to us for a specific ordained purpose. God will breathe on it and use it to His glory, if we surrender to the purpose that He intended. We only need to acknowledge, nurture, develop, and exercise these special abilities. They are to be surrendered to the Lord, and shared with others.

When I said yes to my first ministry job, in addition to a musical gift, I could also read, write, type, and count. These very basic skills may seem insignificant, but when presented to God, miraculous things take place.

Creating a 6,000 name mailing list was my first assigned task. The crusade attendees would fill out an address card. These cards had been gathered for ten years prior to my tenure, and stored in various interesting places. It was now my assignment to locate, organize alphabetically, verify the correct zip codes, and then accurately type each name with the supporting data.

Back then, the ministry didn't own a computer, but we had a typewriter, avery labels, and a three -column alignment guide. A piece of typing paper was placed on the guide, which organized the data into perfect three-column order. Each sheet would be photo copied for storage and the original label used for upcoming ministry events.

This seemingly easy process presented its own set of challenges. As ministry events flourished, and more cards were collected, major adjustments had to be made. Unexpected challenges evolved; address changes, returned mail, bulk mail restrictions, and staff turnover, caused this list to be retyped over six times. Through trial and error and the application of wisdom, we decided to type each list according to zip codes. This directive proved to be a smooth transition from typewriter to a computerized data base.

A beginning typing class was the only official training received prior to this opportunity. Self-doubt was pushed aside as the grace of productivity and proficiency came together. We often wonder why sitting in Math and English classes are so necessary. Those very basic classes teach reasoning applications; necessary tools that fit right into the daily office demands of a growing ministry. With abundant wisdom and a positive attitude, my limited purview was stretched to new horizons. When exposure and interaction, partnered with timing and opportunity, an administrative assistant was born. Basic ministry tasks, developed into broader areas of correspondence, travel arrangements, conference planning, summer tutoring programs, and so much more.

In reflection, I limited my pursuits to music related endeavors, and didn't seek the Lord about my complete career path. My financial situation was unnecessarily strained. The liberating truth was already in my hands. Through trial and error, I learned to pursue through hard work. Sometimes, I was knocked down but never knocked out, knowing that the "purpose" of the Lord would prevail (Proverbs 19:21).

After the ministry job was complete, I pursued other career venues. The work ethic established as a church administrator has positively impacted my success in the hospitality industry for over seventeen years now. Remembering the journey, I indeed realized that "He had already given me what I needed to achieve success." Discarding former habits of comparison, compromise, and procrastination, I pursued with courage, what had already been promised to me. My existing portion, and limited provision, provoked my will to succeed. "Possess and maintain," became my new mantra, motto, and message!

The power of choice, and the will to do what was right, fulfilled a desire to accomplish great things. "I can do all things through Christ which strengthens me" (Phillipians 4:13). Within my inner core, there is a person who wants the best life that can be achieved. I have His word, the Holy Spirit, faith, assurance, wisdom, prophetic insight, and confidence, that" He, who has begun a good

work in me, shall perform it until the coming of the Lord"
(Phillipians 1:6).

James 1:17
Every good and perfect gift is from above
(ASV)

Every good gift bestowed, every perfect gift
received comes to us from above, courtesy of the
Father of lights. He is consistent. He won't change
His mind or play tricks in the shadows…
(VB)

Every desirable and beneficial gift comes out of heaven.
The gifts are rivers of light cascading
down from the Father of Light
(MB)

"Celebrate one day at a time.".
"Enjoy each day of your journey
on the way to your destination…"
Pastor Billy R. Johnson NCCM

You already have what you can handle…..
"Win by Using What is Already in Your Hand!"

✦ Chapter XI ✦

The Servant is the Greatest

"The greatest among you is the servant."
(Matthew 23:11)

"Whoever wants to become great among
you-shall be your servant."
"Whoever wants to be first among you-shall be slave of all."
(Mark 10:42-45)

"Service is the breath and life source of ministry."

Within the vast career spectrum of the hospitality industry, there is one word that summarizes every possible job description, "service." The front desk staff, our first line of service, assists guests with more than mere room accommodations. This is the command center for all guests needs; greeter, listener, mediator, package handler, concierge assistance, and guest accounting.

Our restaurant provides in room dining and room service. The efficient line cooks and exceptional wait staff, bring to life the culinary art of service. From room attendants and housemen, to bellman, agents, and engineers, our guests are wowed with special attention, and personalized care. And when a guest's expectations have not been met, the executive management team handles conflict resolution with precision and excellence.

You may ask yourself, what does the job description of a customer service employee have to do with me? Daily interaction produces some type of service. Whether on the giving or receiving end, it takes great effort, persistence, focus, fortitude, passion, diligence, and sometimes tolerance, to attend to the needs of others. Serving connects us in every stage of life whether in the labor force or in the private sector.

So, how intentional is your will to serve others? Will you only serve as a career minded individual for a prearranged agreement of compensation? Or, will you develop the heart of a servant? The one who intentionally seeks to fulfill "His" purpose in the earth?

• The Role of Service

Matthew 23:11 says "The greatest among you, should be, shall be, will be, must be your minister:

*one who attends to, is
employed by, who performs domestic duties,
the property of, wholly subject to, a bond servant*

In the Strong's Greek concordance entry 1249
The word implied here is…
diakonos(dee-ak'on'os)-servant/minister/deacon…

doulos(doo'los)-the word slave was
never expressed as servant…
(this definition was only translated consistently
in the Holman Christian Bible).
The New Testament usually refers to
the Lord inspiring His servants
to carry out His plan for His people.….

In the Strongs Hebrew concordance entry: 5650..
The word implied here is ebed(eh'-bed)-
Slave, servant, attendant, bondage

• The Mindset of Service

The Hebrew definition takes the idea of service to a more profound level. "Servant" is the equivalent of "slave"; one who was owned or controlled by someone else. The duties of the slave were determined by the owner. They functioned in more than one capacity, and learned to do more than one job. "The greatest among you is the servant"; the one set aside, the slave, the one who does the bidding of the Master, serving where He sees fit.

Slavery was an accepted practice in the Old Testament, but was more humane than that practiced in other ancient civilizations. In biblical times, slaves were the property of their masters with little or no rights or status. This type of slavery, sanctioned in the bible, was very different to that in America in the 17th and 18th centuries. The slavery that the Israelites were subjected to was unacceptable to

God. After the Mosaic Law was given, Israelites were to treat their enslaved as if they were servants and to give a provision for them to make a new start. They could remain slaves if they chose to do so.

•   The Position of Service

(Matthew 6:24 /Luke 16:13)...No one can serve two masters" for either he will hate the one, and love the other; or else he will be devoted to the one and despise the other. You cannot serve both God and money.

You cannot have divided loyalty. Only one will be the greater object of trust, focus, and obedience. In the natural, a slave cannot be physically owned by two masters. All masters have slaves and all slaves have masters. The position of a slave would not exist without a master to rule over them.

In English translations, the word slave carries a stigma. In the New Testament, slave references will only refer to "slaves of sin or slaves of righteousness." On the other hand, this Old Testament Hebrew definition of the word slave shows up 1100 times.

As Christians, we are the children of God, heirs of God and joint heirs with Christ(Romans 8:17) We are members of the body of Christ(Romans 12:5). Jesus is Lord (Kurios). If He is my Lord-then I am His slave.

• **The Posture of Service**

(Matthew 16:23-25 KJV)
Then said Jesus unto his disciples, If any man will come
after me, let him *deny himself,* and *take up his cross,* and
follow me. For whosoever will save his life shall lose it:
and whosoever will lose his life for my sake shall find it.

When you become a believer, you become a slave of
Jesus; His will-His way-His purpose. Our total obedience
transcends and transforms us into another state. So we are
live-in, assigned, assistants, attendants, helpers, domestics,
and serfs, to the work of the Lord. We don't turn off our
duties of service with the buzzing of a time clock. An
efficient servant will always perform the job that needs to
be done. Service is not only an action, but an attitude as
well. A servant is not selective, nor prejudice, but serves
everyone.

• **The Motive of Service**

"Selflessness"
kindness, benevolence, charity,
philanthrophy, humanitarianism

Service provides many opportunities; to share, to
listen, and to be present, fulfilling whatever is needed. I
remember my mother teaching me as a child, that if I only
had a crumb, I should share it with my sister. Morsels of
compassion, patience, wisdom, and unconditional love,
are all examples of that crumb that my mother taught

me to share many years ago. This expression of service far surpasses any family tie, but is extended to everyone that crosses my route, or who may stumble upon my path.

Many will receive what you share with great expectation, but few will reciprocate the gesture when the tables are turned. Sometimes, it may seem that you can't find anyone as liberal as yourself. During these times, the true state of your heart will be revealed as your motive for service is tested and challenged.

Keep your focus on giving excellent service. Continue to serve anyone, anytime, anywhere, in anything, in spite of the response. The reward just may come from someone whom you don't even know. "And the sons of strangers shall build up your walls" (Isaiah 60:10).

- Serving develops a sense of character and self-respect.
- Serving develops proficiency and knowledge of your craft.
- Serving develops self-assurance and stability
- Selflessness opens the door to expand the elevation for others' possibilities
- Serve others as you would have them serve you.
- Serve and consider another before you promote your own needs.
- Serve by showing unlimited examples of hospitality.
- Serving others teaches patience, which can only grow with our cooperation….

- Serving allows you to keep your word, which should be your bond.
  - To minister is to serve.
  - A servant is reliable, dependable, adaptable, accountable, and trustworthy

- **The Transition of Service**

In the book of John Chapter 15:14-15, Jesus said" You are my friends if you do what I command you to do. I no longer call you slaves (servants), because a master doesn't confide in his slaves. Now, you are my friends, since I have told you everything the Father told me (NLT).

Faithful service and commitment is rewarded when trust has been established. When our role, mindset, position, posture, and motive of service, has been proven, another tier of transition unfolds for the slave/servant. With this in mind, the worker moves from the outer circle to the inner circle, and the servant/slave becomes the friend."

If You Want to be Great, Win by Serving!

An assignment is an appointed task,
to fulfill the Great Commission.
With a pre-ordained charge, He will lovingly ask,
then proceed to place you in position.

The purpose of the mission
determines the placement,
inspite of your present condition.
After opposition, trials, adjustments, and tests,
the prep will upgrade your position.

The mission is sure,
The responsibility great,
The potential for discomfort,
The burden carries an eternal weight.

The call to Salvation,
His mission to all.
He gave His own life,
to prevent man's eternal fall.

And then at the end
He will call you to rest.
Enter into His kingdom,
Sit at His feet and be blessed.

Chapter XII

Recognize Your Assignment

In the same way that you gave me a mission in the world,
I give them a mission in the world.
(John 17:18 MSG)

"It Requires a Process"
A series of changes taking place in a definite manner,
development, procedure, formation, course of action.

At the ripe old age of eleven, I remember an insatiable hunger, and an unquenchable thirst, to become a great Gospel Organist. Music was my passion back then, and I pursued it with the precision of a blood hound hunting for his prey. Throughout junior and senior high, and beyond college, I continued to develop my craft. After finishing college, I accepted a teaching position; Vocal Music and Basic English 10, and also taught private piano, organ, and voice lessons. Expanding into recording jingles, song writing and other studio projects, I experienced multiple setbacks and disappointments.

On six separate occasions, the opportunity to record my original songs transpired. The music was recorded, but each time, the masters were never mixed, CD's were never pressed, and the projects were never released. The grace to succeed and the timing of God just didn't culminate success in this arena.

"It Demands Many Adjustments"
correction, modification

Over time, I learned to hear clear precise directives. I became more intentional, pliable, and patient, as He beckoned me toward purpose and destiny. Several distinct incidents transpired as the primary focus of my life began to shift from music to ministry.

The first altering experience was when I had an open vision of myself behind a microphone. At this juncture in life, I was shy and didn't talk in public very much at all. This was a subtle implication of an innovative change. Up to this point, the extent of my public speaking had been limited to choir rehearsal, teaching students in a classroom setting, and private instruction. My response to any other inquiries had been, "I don't speak in public. I only speak at choir rehearsal!"

Several other signposts shifted the course of my life into an adventure. This was far from the familiar definition of normal that I had been accustomed to. While attending a music workshop, a scripture fell into my spirit, "The words that I give you are spirit and they are life"(John 6:63). One Sunday after service, I leaned across the organ to rest a bit. I heard the Holy Spirit speaking to me saying, "*Those hands* are for healing."

Another incident occurred while playing for a revival in New Orleans. The minister looked at me and said "God called you for more than just sitting behind an organ." I had been very comfortable behind the Hammond B-3. So the next few words shook me up a bit. He said that the Lord was going to take me from behind the organ and place me in front of people. I was a bit surprised, yet relieved. The answer to several years of questions was unfolding right before my eyes. All of these subtle encounters were just confirmation. The vision, seeing myself behind a microphone, forever branded in my brain and in my heart.

"It Anticipates Transition"
conversion, evolution, growth, passage,
shift, transformation, turning point

Progressively over time, I began to function administratively, operating proficiently with skills that I didn't know existed. I composed thoughts for the week in our church bulletin, and became a regular teacher for the mid-week bible study. These weekly thoughts turned into chapters culminating in my first book, "Saints, Survival, Kit." My writing skills were further enhanced and several unique sermons were birthed. Then the ultimate opportunity unfolded. I compiled an Old and New Testament training course for our School of

Ministry and another manual for our Worship and Arts Department.

A renewed interest in the area of math was rekindled, expanding into two other career paths; night auditor and math tutor. I was also asked to compile a training manual for our department at work. Just as confirmation would have it, I was indeed in front of a microphone, far away from the B-3 organ that I had been so comfortable with.

Life happened, experiences unfolded, living arrangements shifted, and uncharted territories were encountered. I didn't pen anything for the next fifteen years. Finally from 2010 to 2016, I completed three more literary offerings of inspired thoughts; "The Cost of the Win" Part I and II, and "Study Tips from A to Z".

This present connection to a literary career is so surreal. My Grandmother started piano lessons with me at age five. My one desire was to be a full-time musician, and travel the world. That is what I pursued, and that is what I went after; including the traveling part. But somewhere between pursuing my goals and being obedient to the assignment, I became a writer.

It is ironic that my focus has shifted from music to ministry but the transition is sweet. My passion to play has been replaced by a desire to study, write, and share my experiences. If anyone had told me over forty years ago that I would not function as a musician, I probably would've laughed just like Sarah did in disbelief. Thank God for His patience with us as we allow His will and His way of doing things to transform us.

"It Ultimately Creates Purpose"
The reason for which something exists.

For we are his workmanship, created in
Christ Jesus for good works,
which God prepared beforehand, that
we should walk in them.
(Ephesians 2:10)

So many times we pass through life encountering opportunities that promote growth and spiritual maturity. Instead of celebrating the conditioning process, we tend to focus on the discomfort. Daily challenges and annoying trials bring us to a wealthy place (Psalms 66:12). Our steps have been ordered (Psalms 37:23). We are not living by accident, fluke, or coincidence. Everything that collides with our route has intent. Every opportunity that influences our path has purpose. Not only are the pleasant encounters good for us, but the confrontational venues are prime resources as well.

We have been preordained" to be conformed" to the image of Christ. There is a scripture that says, "Thou He was a son, yet He learned obedience through the things He suffered"(Hebrews 5:8). Our assignment is the catalyst that gets us to that place of total surrender. It starts with process, demands adjustments, requires transition, and culminates with the fulfillment of purpose in our lives (II Timothy 1:9).

God has a plan for each of us. Many choose to walk in their own selfish pursuits. They are governed by the poll of popular opinion, as if it was a democratic election.

I can't tell you how many times I've heard," I wouldn't do that!" You're giving up too much! Why do you work so hard!! Others have tried to discourage me from doing what I know the Lord is leading me to do. Just keep the main thing, the main thing. Recognize that this is your assignment. He didn't tell them, He told you!

While dining with some family members recently, I began to share some of the most colorful-unexpected experiences encountered on the road. I finally realized that the courage to endure, and making wise choices, developed maturity, stability, integrity, and character within me. For many years, I admired others who seemed to be more gifted, grounded, and experienced. A cruel awakening surfaced. Their gifts had taken them to places where their character could not sustain them. Having missed the ordained assignment, they wasted precious time to pursue unproductive endeavors. Unable to yield to the one who initially called them, they never got back on track.

"Faith not tested cannot be trusted."

I remember hearing a wise old man say, "He never promised us a gravy train with biscuit wheels". Even though He equips us, trains us, and points us in the right direction, there are major challenges and many times of great opposition. "Of much is given, much is required" (Luke 12:36). We must learn to work through it and not quit. You must remember, "We are learning His ways!"

As you learn, you must allow others to learn as well! This tempers us, conditions us, and establishes us in the ordained path. The acquisition is so much sweeter when we learn to "yield to", rather than "fight against" the process.

My hands are indeed healing people with my words, whether in printed form or via audio books. I must say, I am a willing participant and really enjoying the journey. I recognize the leading of the Lord, then yield to it! My journey has been an example of process, leading to adjustments, which causes transition, to places unknown. The fulfillment of purpose is just the by- product of engaging in the ultimate assignment.

Purpose does not discriminate when the assignment seems small. "The greatest among you is the servant." He only requires us to give of ourselves. Our time, talent, and resources will follow as good stewards, wherever we go. We should extend ourselves beyond what we can see and value others above ourselves. We must sacrifice our comfort for the comfort of others, so expect to be inconvenienced sometimes. We must suffer loss to gain; to be, to thrive, to live, to survive.

It begins with "Process."
It demands "Adjustments."
It requires "Transition."
It precedes "Purpose."

"Win by Recognizing Your Assignment!"

FAVORABLE

ADORNING

VICTORIOUS

OVER-FLOWING

REGARD

✦ Chapter XIII ✦

Favor vs Fair

"Noah found favor in the eyes of the Lord"
(Genesis 6:8)
It wasn't fair that he was ridiculed, taunted,
and teased, for building the Ark in a
place where rain had never been experienced
before. But his obedience and God's
favor preserved his entire family.

*"But the Lord was with Joseph and
extended kindness to him,
and gave him favor in the sight of the chief jailer"*
(Genesis 39:21)
It was not fair that Joseph was sold by his brothers,
lied on by Potaphar's wife, and put in prison.
But His great discomfort was the catalyst that
eventually preserved his family in the time of
famine. It caused an entire nation of people to exist,
fulfilling a promise to Abraham to become the
"Father of many nations"

*"Now the boy Samuel was growing in stature and in favor
both with the Lord and with men"*
(I Samuel 2:26)

Hannah, dedicated Samuel to the service of the
Lord. Her response to fulfill a promise, caused the
favor of God to reign over his entire life. He became
a great priest, prophet, and judge. He was a wise
leader, very rich, and committed to the service of
God. Samuel was a true example of faithfulness and
honesty to his calling and to the people of his day.

"For he who finds me, finds life and
obtains favor from the Lord"
(Proverbs 8:35)

"And Jesus kept increasing in wisdom and stature,
and in favor with God and men"
(Luke 2:52)

"The Lord make His face shine on
you, and be gracious to you"
(Numbers 6:25)

"For You are the glory of their strength,
and by Your favor our horn is exalted"
(Psalm 89:17)

Many are focused on only receiving what is fair versus
living under the abundant favor of the Lord. It is fair to
get a paycheck at the end of a forty-hour work week. But
it is so rewarding to receive a promotion for a position that

you are not qualified for, after working at a company for a short time. This is favor!

Yes, it is fair when you are approved for a house or apartment, because you have good credit score. But it is favor when you need to downsize within two short weeks. Quickly acquiring a suitable dwelling place, you receive the keys, without a credit check, or a security deposit. This is favor!

When it is time to move in, it is fair to rent a truck, and have all of the prearranged manpower needed to help you move. But sometimes you don't have enough help. Favor brings a stranger to your front door on a Monday, to view the house that you are leaving. The stranger just happens to have their own U-Haul truck, and three sons, who offer to move the rest of your stuff the very next day. Then agree to wait until the end of the week, to receive payment. This is favor!

It is fair to expect your car to be repossessed for multiple months of non-payment. But it is favor when the loan company accepts your payment arrangement, stopping the repossession process. Favor supports a sigh of relief, when you refuse to be stressed while feeling the weight of the world on your shoulders. "Favor" isn't fair, but it sure benefits the believer, who is totally depending on God to intervene in pressure situations.

Favor in Hebrew means grace-adornment

Favor is Grace:
- the free unmerited love and favor of God

- the spring and source of all the benefits men receive from Him
  - favorable influence of God
- divine influence of the spirit, renewing the heart, and restraining from sin

Favor is Charis:
forgiveness of sins- access-power

Favor is Assistance:
backing, benefit, consideration, gift, respect, support
special accommodation, cooperation, esteem, grace,
kindness, partiality, patronage, regard

Fair
- free from bias, equal, impartial
- legitimate, reasonable, nonpartisan
- square, straight, even-handedness

- good sportsmanship
- follow and play by the rules
- don't make waves
- do the expected thing, to get the expected result

"Live in His favor
not in the paradox of fairness."

Favor is limitless;
It stretches the boundaries, and expands
the territory of possibilities.

"Win with the Favor of the Lord!"

Chapter XIV

Reflections

In Part One of The Cost of the Win, I dealt with positional changes. These key elements are crucial to the success of any potential winner. Whether pursuing educational achievements, a specific career path, or a higher calling to ministry of any kind we must learn to:

- triumph over fear by making adjustments to change
- be courageous in the face of the unknown
- be willing to prepare in private for public display
- tackle impatience by exercising patience in every situation
- experience the loss of a loved one and still celebrate with joy
- tap into His frequency and respond to His voice
- train our will by persistent conditioning of our minds

In Part II of The Cost of the Win, I
dealt with His vehicle for success;
provision for the assignment, and tools for successful
achievement. These special agents are assigned
to assist, with the completion of our task.

- Daily Bread-Daily Benefits advantageous benefits on a daily basis.

- Responsibility Breeds Maturity reliability, dependability, accountability, brings full development.

- What I Need Is Already in My Hand possessed, owned, and grasped within my reach.

- The Servant is the Greatest notable, remarkable, exceptional.

- Recognize Your Assignment identify it, perceive it, acknowledge it.

- Favor; preferential treatment supercedes

Fair; a proper recompence determined
by merely following rules.

--SUMMARY--

The art of winning has many faces, just like conquering tests and trials result in seizing the victory.

Promotion comes from God but He must equip us to handle the promotion. Continue to remind yourself that what you are presently facing is not a punishment but a promotion! Push past the barriers! You are winning on multiple levels and at every stage of development.

While writing this book I suffered two major setbacks. After six years of research and compiling data on two USB ports, while sitting with my mother at the hospital I lost my purse. I only had a few pages printed and the Lord changed the entire format of the book into the form that you are experiencing today. At first glance, winning was nowhere in sight, but He lead me around the obstacle to finish this race.

The next challenge happened as recently Monday, 11-13-18. While trying to finish the final edits to send to the publisher for Book II, I broke the USB port with all of the final edits and updates. Yes, I learned from the first time and had a backup port in my home safe with all six projects on it. But the updates were not on the backup port. Immediately, I encouraged myself that after the first incident, the Lord caused me to rewrite a better manuscript the second time around. This opportunity would be no different. The Holy Spirit would bring back what I needed and would lead me to other ideas to enhance what was lost. This mission was accomplished and the edits for Book II were rewritten. Then He reminded me that I had previously emailed the edits for Book I to the publisher. I found them in the sent items and rejoiced that they were still intact!

At first glance it looked rather bleak, but in the midst of this challenge, I've learned to look toward other avenues to complete the assigned task. He came through for me and I matured in the process. This project has cost me a lot, but I still win!

When we say yes to salvation, the path to obedience takes us to routes unknown. The process is sometimes very difficult and uncomfortable, but the rewards are great, and very beneficial. You have been bought with a price and are no longer your own (I Corinthians 6:20). The reward is with Him and in Him. We win because He has already won!!!

This encounter began with a focus on challenge. I've moved from challenge to transition, from focus to a change of mindset, and from idle responses to a secure status of faith. I now welcome the unknown, and have learned to pursue without fear. When cherishing opportunities, anticipating possibilities, forgiving as I follow on to know the Lord, and wearing the world like a loose garment, I now reach beyond my reach. Always remembering:

- there is a price to pay
- a value assigned,
- premiums in the form of experience gained,
- assessment of lessons learned,
- reward for journeys completed,

And a Cost Attached to Every Win!!!

*Thank You for Sharing in My Journey
and in the Discovery of What it Cost to Win!!!
Tamara Lofton*

About the Author

Tamara accepted the Lord as "Savior and Lord of her life" at age eighteen, but in reflection, she hadn't acknowledged Him about what her total career path should be. Coming from a lineage of educators, she also decided to be a teacher. Music was all that she knew; piano lessons since age four, played for churches since age twelve, trained choirs at age fifteen, went to college as a Music Ed major, studied voice, became a High School music teacher, wrote gospel songs and commercial jingles, and traveled for thirteen years as an organist for an evangelist.

She had chosen music, but He had another plan. Somewhere between learning to yield to His purpose, and doing life, something changed! The Lord breathed life into dormant gifts, using her in areas that she had not been professionally trained in. A love for music transitioned into a passion for the word. Basic reading, writing, math, and typing skills, became the catalyst. A genuine love for people surfaced. Her focus changed, and she connected, by becoming a tutor of music, math, and the message of Christ. An author and administrator was born, replacing the career path that she had previously chosen for herself.

Tamara is a member of New Covenant Christian Ministries in Lithonia, Ga. pastored by, Pastor Billy R. and Dr. D'Ann Johnson. She has served in several capacities; minister, worship & arts, voice over announcer, and facilitator for school of ministry, discipleship, and small groups classes.

Contact the Author

Mailing Address
P.O. Box 239
Stone Mountain, GA 30086

Email
tamrhythmic@yahoo.com

Projects are Available in:
Soft Cover, E-Books, Audio Books

The Cost of the Win Part I
The Cost of the Win Part II
Saints Survival Kit

Audio Versions Only:

Trust and Don't Trip

Your Temptation;
Are You Affected By It or Infected With It?

A Functioning Vessel or a Vessel of Purpose?
Study Tips from A to Z

Printed in the United States
By Bookmasters